Let's Discuss

WOMEN'S RIGHTS

Barbara Einhorn

Let's Discuss

First published in 1988 by
Wayland (Publishers) Ltd
61 Western Road, Hove
East Sussex BN3 1JD, England

Editor: Jannet King
Designer: Ross George

British Library Cataloguing in Publication Data
Einhorn, Barbara
  Let's discuss women's rights. – (Let's discuss).
  1. Women – Great Britain – Social conditions
  I. Title
  305.4′2′0941   HQ1593

  ISBN 1–85210–111–3

Typeset by Kalligraphics Ltd
Redhill, Surrey
Printed and bound in the UK at
The Bath Press, Avon

Front cover: *Women workers at a Ford plant fighting for equal pay. How far have women come in their struggle for equal rights, and how much further do they have to go?*

Contents

The case studies in this book are fictitious. They are not subject to copyright and may be reproduced for use in the classroom.

Introduction: What Are Women's Rights?

What does it mean when we talk about women's rights? Do they differ from men's rights? Or from human rights in general? Many people argue that women should have equal opportunities to those which men enjoy, but that they do not get them without a struggle.

From the eighteenth century until about 100 years ago, a woman was thought of as her husband's property. He owned all her possessions, her earnings, and even her children. A wife had no legal rights at all. In Victorian times, women had little choice about what they would be. Between 1875 and 1900, one in every three girls between the ages of fifteen and twenty was a domestic servant. If they were 'lucky', women were married off to a 'good match', or became governesses if they had some education themselves, but many women worked twelve hours a day in factories such as textile mills or brickworks.

Diane Abbott, Britain's first black woman MP, at the declaration of the election results in her constituency in June 1987, nearly seventy years after women were given the vote.

The slogan 'A Woman's Right to Choose' is as relevant today as it was in October 1979 when these placards were carried on a demonstration to protest against a private member's bill to reform the abortion law.

Throughout the twentieth century, women have been involved in women's rights movements. The suffragettes wanted the right to vote. Other groups thought that better conditions for the many women working long hours in the factories were more important than political rights. The women's movement of the 1970s and 1980s has had many different groups working within it, for the right to abortion, the right of working women to have their children cared for during the day, protection for women who are beaten and badly treated by their husbands, or for the recognition of gay rights.

Rights mean different things to different groups. And everyone sees women's problems from their own point of view. As a teacher and writer, I cannot speak for the needs of women working in factories or stores, or homeless women, perching with their children in bed-and-breakfast accommodation. Nor can I speak for the black and Asian women of this country who have to suffer the double problems of racism as well as sexism, as prejudice against women is sometimes called. Just as every book you read is written from the perspective of one particular author, so every woman speaks with her own voice. In this book, you will be getting my views of the issue of women's rights.

The right to live with your family may seem fundamental, but some women have difficulty arranging this. When Salema Begum's parents came to Britain she stayed in Bangladesh with her grandmother. Now that her grandmother has died Salema wishes to live with her parents and came here on a visit. The Home Office first said she had to return to Bangladesh, prove her parentage and reapply for admission. Then they allowed her to do the necessary blood tests in this country. Here she is shown with her father in Chorlton Central Church which gave her sanctuary.

Of all the groups fighting for women's rights, none take it to mean that women and men should be the same, or even equal in everything. Women want the opportunity to develop their full potential. Women's rights is about equal opportunities to achieve this wish.

1 Think of some examples from your school or home life where girls are treated differently from boys.
2 When someone says 'typical woman' when referring to a female driver or a woman changing her mind about something, what do they mean?
3 Many scholars throughout history have argued that women are, by nature, inferior to men. Discuss this view.

Discuss the view that 'women all over the world have less power, less autonomy, more work, less money, and more responsibility', from Women in the World: An International Atlas (Pluto Press, 1986)

Fighting For Rights: Suffragettes and Women Workers

Today we take it for granted that everyone over the age of eighteen can vote. So it is hard for us to imagine that it took well over fifty years of struggle to win this right for women. The National Union of Women's Suffrage Societies was formed in 1861. During the 1890s, a working woman called Selina Cooper helped to raise the issue of women's suffrage in the trade unions in Manchester. With other women, she built a mass movement based on the Lancashire cotton mills. The radical suffragists, as this group was called, saw the right to vote as a way of improving living and working conditions for factory women like themselves.

The movement of women's suffrage was very broad. The best-known group were the suffragettes. They belonged to the Women's Social and Political Union, founded in Manchester in 1903 by Mrs Emmeline Pankhurst. Her daughter, Christabel, and Annie Kenney, one of the few working-class women in the WSPU, were thrown out of a Liberal Party rally in 1905 after they had hung a white banner and shouted out its slogan of 'Votes for Women'. After their arrest the two women went to prison rather than pay a fine. The Pankhursts moved to London in 1906 and continued to campaign, using street demonstrations, meetings in Hyde Park, and increasingly dramatic and spectacular tactics to attract attention to their cause. This was the only way they felt they could get publicity and force the politicians to listen to their demands. The suffragettes endured many hardships as a result of their campaigns. Many of them were repeatedly put in prison and force-fed when they went on hunger-strike in support of their demand to be classed as political prisoners rather than as common criminals.

Suffragettes being led away after a demonstration. The number of policemen shows that the suffragettes posed a serious threat to the authorities of the day.

Women, called 'munitionettes', preparing shell heads during the First World War. Much of the work done by women in the munitions factories was dangerous and had long-term ill-effects on their health.

The radical suffragists back in Lancashire felt the Pankhursts and their group were élitist. Selina Cooper was one of the many who disapproved of their violent tactics. And unlike the Lancashire women, the WSPU certainly did seem to view the vote as an end in itself. Mrs Pankhurst wrote that WSPU members 'are absolutely single-minded . . . no member of the WSPU divides her attention between suffrage and other social reforms.'

Votes for women were finally won in two stages. After millions of men volunteered to fight in the First World War, women took over their jobs. Over a million women did dangerous work in the munitions factories. Others became bus drivers, porters and window cleaners, worked on the land and in shipyards, drove ambulances, lorries and motor bikes. By 1918, almost 2 million women were working in men's jobs. In February 1918, women over 30 who were married or householders were given the right to vote, but it was not until 1928, when all women over the age of 21 were entitled to vote, that they achieved political equality with men.

Having the vote did not stop 750,000 of the 7,333,000 women in employment losing their jobs when the men came back from the war. Women were forced to go back into their homes or into other people's as domestic servants again. By 1928, domestic service accounted for 35 per cent of all women workers, just as it had done in 1911. But because of the demanding and often dangerous work they had done during the war, women had gained a new independence and confidence.

In the Second World War women were actually conscripted into the services or war work but again, at the end of the war, their jobs were reclaimed by men.

Women working on the docks during the First World War. Although they are wearing trousers for work, it was not until the Second World War that trousers became accepted as leisure wear for women.

Case Study 1:

Molly, aged 73

The bombing raids were terrible for those living in London, but Molly loved the war years. She lived in Liverpool and worked down the shipyard, riveting metal sheets for ship repairs. Her team was almost completely made up of women, so there was plenty of company. And her children were well looked after in the local council nursery. It was only just down the road from where Molly lived, so it didn't take long to take the children there in the morning and fetch them on the way home. The staff were very kind, and the place was nice and sunny. Really, Bobby and Sheila were better off there than at home – more toys to play with, loads of little playmates – and a good hot dinner in the middle of the day.

The only thing that wasn't so good was the news, and the waiting every day, hoping that Stuart was safe out there in the fighting and would soon be back on leave. But it was good to share your worries with the other girls during the tea break, and not to be stuck at home on your own. Besides she was earning a good wage. And the work might be tough, but it was a challenge she enjoyed. To think that the men had always gone on about it being 'men's work', that women were too weak to hold the tools, and too silly and frightened to be able to work high up.

In a funny way, it was much harder when the war ended in 1945. The first thing that happened was that she lost her job at the shipyard. The only thing she could find instead was a job answering the telephone in a lawyer's office in town. The pay was only half what she had been getting as a riveter, and her boss spoke to her as if she was mentally retarded. And when Stuart finally got demobbed, he thought everything at home would be decided on his say-so – after she'd been alone all those years, having to make all the decisions about the children, and managing on the ration cards too.

Then when little Peter should have gone to the nursery, in 1950, they closed it down and started saying a woman's place was at home with the kids. When it suited them to have the women go out to work because the country would have collapsed without them, they were full of praise for nurseries, saying it gave the kids social contact no mother could possibly provide. What made them think they could march back home and take over the place, giving orders to all their womenfolk?

Many women joined the Auxilliary Territorial Services (ATS) during the Second World War and some became lorry drivers.

1 What do you think of the tactics the suffragettes used, like chaining themselves to the railings outside Parliament? Do you feel this is the only way for women to be noticed, and hence to be effective, in gaining rights nowadays?

2 Was Molly right to feel resentful when she lost her job after the Second World War? It is still true today that women are the first to lose their jobs?

Are childcare facilities like nurseries a good thing for children, or are they better off at home? Discuss the view that 'children's emotional and intellectual development can be badly affected by spending time in nurseries. They need their mothers' attention until the age of 5'. And is a mother the only parent who can give children the type of love and care they need?

The Women's Liberation Movement

The earliest women's movements fought for women's legal and political rights. The Women's Liberation Movement which began in the late 1960s was more concerned to find out *why* women were oppressed. In the early consciousness-raising groups, women shared their personal experiences and began to piece together a new story. While some groups within the movement still felt that the most important thing was to change laws and to get more women into politics so that they could influence the decision-making process, many others discussed the private as well as public ways in which women were dominated and humiliated in their everyday lives. These included discrimination at school, unequal pay, poor working conditions and often sexual harassment at work, portrayal as sex objects in newspapers and magazines, advertisements and TV, and violent treatment at home. Under the slogan of 'the personal is political', the WLM brought many issues into public discussion for the first time. As well as setting up self-help women's centres and campaigning for childcare facilities, they set up refuges for battered wives and rape crisis centres to help and counsel women victims of male violence.

In the 1960s there were demonstrations calling for equal pay, equal education, equal job opportunities and free childcare.

These demonstrators were demanding the release of four women and a gay man arrested after the women had gone to the assistance of the man who was being attacked in the street.

Within the women's movement, the discussion continues to rage as to who is to blame for women's oppression: is it capitalism and the class system which exploits women, or is it the system of domination by men known as patriarchy? In the twenty years of its history the movement has divided into various groups, sometimes to campaign around single issues, such as the Abortion Campaign, sometimes around the theoretical debates. Socialist feminists were more concerned with the economic ways in which women were exploited, so some of them felt able to organize together with men to change the whole structure of society. An early success was to persuade the trade unions in 1974 to adopt a Working Women's Charter. Those concerned with legal rights saw the Equal Pay Act of 1970, the Sex Discrimination Act of 1975 and the establishment of an Equal Opportunities Commission in 1975 as major victories.

But many feminists felt it was necessary for women to organize separately from men, in order to find their own voice and have the strength to change things for women. Working in the unions and in political parties in the 1960s, many women felt they did not have the courage to speak up at meetings, and that the men actually expected them mainly to address envelopes and make the tea. Some feminists – the radical separatists – felt so bitter about the growing evidence of men's violence towards women that they did not wish to work with men at all.

The first women's liberation conference in Oxford in 1970 formulated four demands which still stand today: for equal pay, for equality of education and opportunity, for 24-hour nurseries, and for free contraception and abortion on demand. Later, the Working Women's Charter of 1974 formulated ten demands linking women's roles at home and at work. With the development of the Gay Rights movement, the demand for a woman's right to define her own sexuality and for an end to discrimination against lesbians was added. These demands, together with those for financial and legal independence, for freedom from intimidation by the threat or use of violence and an end to male aggression and dominance, are still current in today's women's movement.

The tactics used by the suffragettes have influenced all popular movements in the twentieth century. In the same way the WLM has had an effect beyond the issues themselves. As a reaction to being dominated by men, women have devized a non-hierarchical structure for their organizations: there are no leaders and all women have an equal voice in decision-making. This approach has changed forever the way people relate to each other in political parties and other campaigning organizations.

1   Do you think that when girls and boys meet in separate groups they talk about things they don't talk about in mixed groups? If so, why do you think this is?
2   Do you know anyone who is bullied because of their preference for people of the same sex? What is your view about this?
3   Do you think that views about women's role in society have changed much since your parents were young? Compare what you know about the way they were brought up and educated and their attitudes today with your own and those of your friends.

Some feminists think that women will only be treated as equal to men if more of them gain positions of power, such as becoming MPs, judges or managers. Others think that it is more important for women to change the views and behaviour of the men they live and work with. What do you think?

Educating Women

From a very early age, girls are trained to conform to a stereotyped image of what it is to be a woman. Mothers pass on what their mothers told them: that girls are not only biologically different from boys, but should act differently and have different expectations of life. By the time they get to nursery school, girls and boys play differently and separately. Playground games at primary school are usually very separate for boys and girls. This division is reinforced by organized school sports: boys play football – the most glamorous sport in the land, watched by millions – while girls play netball.

The separation between boys and girls grows much wider at secondary school, where they often study different subjects. But even in infant school, most of the reading schemes and children's books show more boys than girls, and it is usually the boys who have the adventures.

A little girl dresses up as mother to play with her dolls.

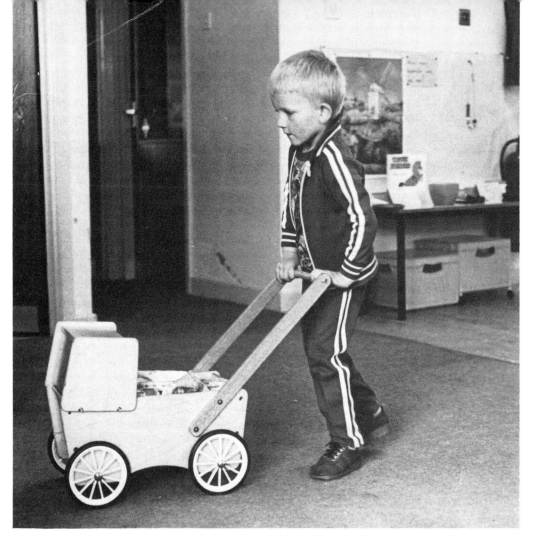

Only a few nursery schools encourage boys to play with dolls. If more boys were given this childhood experience they might be better able to care for their own children when they grow up.

It is hard to know whether girls decide as a result of these early lessons that they are 'no good at maths', or whether teachers advise them to take French rather than physics, home economics rather than woodwork or metal-work. Often the curriculum is structured in such a way that such choices are hard to avoid, and teachers may not even be aware of how much they influence girls and boys to choose diferent subjects.

'O' level examination results show clear evidence of these gender divisions. In 1984, 60,000 boys sat 'O' level French compared with over 90,000 girls. But only 16,600 girls took 'O' level computer studies compared with 39,000 boys. Who has decided that computer studies is not a subject for girls, and why? Perhaps the connection with maths is important. Not only do many fewer girls than boys take an 'O' level in maths, but fewer of those girls who sit the exam pass it. The same pattern occurs with computer studies. Girls who do take computer studies or other "boys'" subjects often feel that their questions are not dealt with seriously in class. They feel the teacher assumes they are stupid or incapable of understanding the subject. This is borne out by the remark made by a secondary school physics teacher in 1981 (quoted by Juliet McCaffery in *What about Women?*): 'Boys are more interested in science than girls. They ask better questions too.' And even in marking practice there is evidence of prejudice against girls. When the same exam papers were marked with a candidate's number on them rather than their name, many more girls passed than when their names were on the papers.

Many feminists have argued that girls do better in all-girls schools, and examination results prove them right. Statistics quoted in *The Guardian* on 22 October 1987 show that girls in girls' grammar schools did better at 'O' level than both girls and boys in other schools. Perhaps co-educational comprehensives should introduce single-sex classes for maths and science subjects to give girls equal educational opportunities.

Research has shown that girls in single-sex schools do better at sciences than when they are competing with boys in co-educational schools.

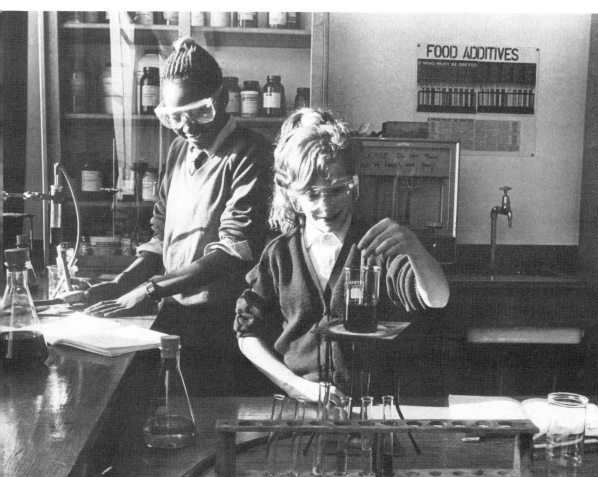

Case Study 2:

Jill, aged 25

Jill went to a mixed comprehensive school. She was quite good at science and thought she might like to do something in engineering. But when she spoke to her year head about subject choices for her 'O' level exams, he advised her against doing all three sciences. He said it would be very hard for her to get into engineering and would take a long time to train. Besides, she might well just end up getting married, and then all that effort would be wasted. He advised her to stick to French and typing. That would get her a good secretarial job.

Jill was determined. She stuck to her choice and took all three sciences. 'It was tough going,' she recalls, 'not because the work was too difficult, but because the boys gave me a hard time. It doesn't pay to be good at science subjects if you want to be popular.'

In her 'O' level year, Jill went to see the careers advice teacher to ask about a career in engineering. He gave her a funny look and said: 'Engineering isn't for girls. Be sensible. You don't want to go round covered in grease all day, do you?' Jill felt angry, but when she discussed it at home her parents agreed with him. In any case, they said they couldn't afford to go on supporting her. She would have to leave school after this year and go out to work.

Jill felt very disheartened. Perhaps the adults were right. She set about looking through job advertisements without much enthusiasm. Even with 'O' levels there didn't seem to be much she could do. Suddenly she spotted an ad which had on it: 'We are an equal opportunities employer.' And it was with a local engineering firm!

Two years later Jill was doing so well as a lathe operator that her boss suggested she apply to the local technical college to do a course in mechanical engineering. When she was accepted, her firm gave her one day a week off to go to college. The course was great. The only problem was the boys: 'I felt I had to do twice as well as them to prove I could do it,' said Jill.

Most of the workers in her firm are men, but they respect her skill. 'I think they accept me now' she says. 'If something goes wrong; it's me they come to for advice.' Jill is saving hard, hoping to buy a flat with her boyfriend. And she has other plans too: 'I'd like to go on to university if I can,' she says, 'to do a degree in electronic engineering. I feel there are more career opportunities in that branch of engineering these days.'

A civil engineer working for British Rail.

1 What are the arguments against girls playing football? Do you agree with them? Could you imagine netball becoming a national sport which people watch on TV?

2 Should it be compulsory for all schoolchildren to study chemistry and French, woodwork and cooking? What difference would this make?

3 'Little girls don't play with cars. It is cissy for little boys to play with dolls.' How many times have you heard this sort of thing said to small children?

Discuss the view recently expressed by the admissions tutor for a Cambridge University college: 'Academically there is more of a tendency for women to underperform, wherever they are, than men.'

Women's Work

'A woman's work is never done' goes the old saying, and in some senses this is more true today than ever. Modern appliances make housework easier, but it is still mainly women who do it. A survey quoted in *The Guardian* on 20 June 1987 found that women spend on average 39 hours a week on housework. Yet women also account for 46 per cent of all employees and well over half of all married women go out to work. For them, this results in what feminists have called the 'double burden': paid work *plus* housework and childcare.

The idea, still taught to girls at home, in school and through women's magazines and the media, that a woman's main occupation is as a wife and mother just does not fit reality. In 1983, only one in five families conformed to the stereotype image, with dad going out to work and mum staying home to look after two children. Most families depend on the woman's wage as well as what the man earns or gets in unemployment benefit. And for the 830,000 women who are single parents, the family has to live on what they alone earn.

Most women take responsibility for the household chores, and even if they go out to work, they feel guilty if their house is not spotless.

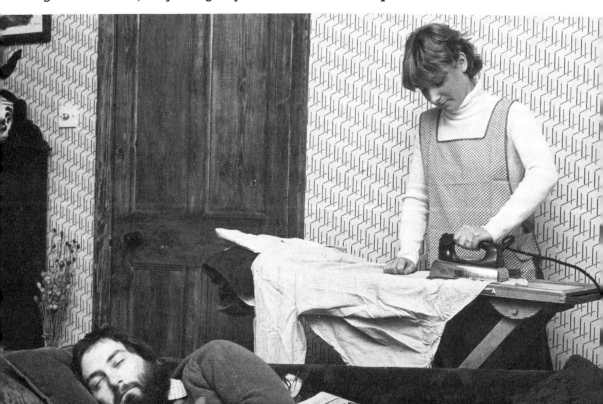

Many women work in small businesses such as this clothing workshop and are not protected by the Equal Pay Act. If they work part-time they have very few employment rights and they are probably paid so little they can't afford to pay someone else to look after their children.

Britain has the lowest number of nursery school places in the whole of Western Europe with only 47 per cent of 4 year olds in nurseries, while France and Belgium have places for 97 per cent of 4 year olds. Most British nurseries look after children for only half a day which means that most women with young children are only able to work part-time or have to depend on neighbours, friends, relatives or paid childminders to look after their children.

Most working women in Britain are employed in a narrow range of jobs. There are very few women lawyers, doctors, accountants or computer analysts and only one in ten engineers and scientists is a woman. Women who work in the professions tend to remain near the bottom of the promotion pyramid. Although there were more than three times as many women primary school teachers as men in 1977, there were fewer women head teachers. In secondary schools there are almost as many women teachers as men, but there are between four and five male head teachers for every woman head.

Women are far more likely to work as cleaners, shop assistants, factory workers, secretaries and typists than in jobs which require more training, perhaps because of the myth that they will only be working temporarily until they marry and have children. The type of work they do is usually poorly paid and dull or repetitive: serving, cleaning, and caring for other people. They tend to have little job satisfaction and often poor career prospects.

Most women do not get equal pay with men, despite the Equal Pay Act of 1970. Because women and men are often in different jobs, it is easy for employers to discriminate against women. The Act itself excludes women who work in private households, such as au-pairs, and women who work for an employer who employs fewer than six people.

More people work part-time in Britain than in most other countries. The 4.95 million part-timers in Britain make up almost half of the 12 million part-timers in all of the EEC. Of these 4.95 million, women account for 4.1 million but the Equal Pay Act, the Sex Discrimination Act, and the Equal Opportunities Commission have done little to help them. The right to appeal against unfair dismissal, to proper holiday and sick pay, redundancy pay and to return to a job after maternity leave, all depend on working sixteen hours per week in the same job for two years, or eight hours per week over five years. It is easy to see how this condition excludes many part-time women. A recent survey by the Low Pay Unit found that British part-timers have the worst pay levels and working conditions in the whole of the EEC.

Part-timers are also easier to sack than full-timers, so in times of economic recession like the present, women are often the first to lose their jobs. Automation and computerisation mean that under-trained and unskilled workers, often women, lose out. Unions – mainly run by men – also tend to protect their full-time members rather than part-timers. Nearly a third of all unemployed people in Britain are women. And since many married women who wish to work are not registered as unemployed, the proportion is probably far higher still.

Although there are comparatively few women barristers, more women are now completing the long training this job requires.

The Cammell Laird cook, Julie Hayward, in October 1984 after she won her case for equal pay for work of equal value with that of her male colleagues elsewhere in the shipyard. But the case went to the Employment Appeals Tribunal and then to the Court of Appeal in March 1987 where it was ruled that she was not owed any money because her other employment terms were more favourable than the men's. She was allowed to take her case to the House of Lords, however, in order to establish this important point.

1   Although women make up almost half the workforce in Britain, and hospitals would collapse without them, many people say women are 'taking away' men's jobs. Discuss this view.
2   In the United States, there are quotas specifying the number of student places and jobs in colleges and universities which should go to women. Do you think there should be a similar quota system in Britain?
3   'No, I don't work – I'm just a housewife'. Why do you think women say this? Is it true?
4   'Until men and women share the burden of housework and childcare equally, women will never have truly equal rights'. Discuss this view.

Women's Health

One of the central issues raised by the Women's Liberation Movement in the 1970s was that women should have a right to free contraception, regardless of their age and marital status, that they should be able to choose how to give birth, and that they should have access to free and legal abortions. In other words, the campaign was about women's right to decide whether and when to have children: 'a woman's right to choose' as the slogan of the National Abortion Campaign (NAC) put it.

All these campaigns have been the subject of much publicity and controversy. In early 1985 Mrs Victoria Gillick won a Court of Appeal ruling banning doctors from giving contraceptive or abortion advice or prescribing contraceptives to girls under the age of sixteen. This led feminists to express fears that more young girls would become pregnant and without advice would be forced to seek back-street abortions to hide their pregnancy from their parents. The Gillick ruling also undermines the important civil right of confidentiality between the doctor and the patient.

Giving birth is a process which many feminists felt had been removed from the control of women themselves. Doctors, mainly male, were making decisions about whether drugs were necessary during labour, or whether a caesarian birth was needed. Midwives, largely women, had to go along with what the doctor said. The person who seemed to have least say was the woman herself. Feminists and other women working together have managed to achieve many changes in hospital practices.

Abortion was illegal in Britain until the passing of the 1967 Act made it possible to have an abortion legally on certain grounds. It is possible to get an abortion for 'social' reasons if two doctors agree. But this process often causes delay, resulting in abortions being carried out later than they ideally should be. Anti-abortion groups like the Society for the Protection of Unborn Children (SPUC) and Life argue that abortion is murder. Many people feel that until a foetus's lungs and other organs are sufficiently developed at about twenty-four weeks to enable it to survive outside the womb, it cannot be called a human life.

Whether contraception is safe is as important an issue as whether it is freely available. The advent of the birth control pill in the 1960s gave women almost 100 per cent protection against unwanted pregnancy. But research during the 1970s and 1980s has given substance to women's claims that the pill can cause many harmful illnesses and unwanted side-effects. Many women have gone back, to the less convenient, but less potentially harmful, diaphragm or Dutch cap because of the links between the pill and cancer of the cervix or the breast. Feminist slogans have expressed the view that if men had to have unwanted babies or abortions, they would have put resources into finding safe and effective forms of birth control long ago.

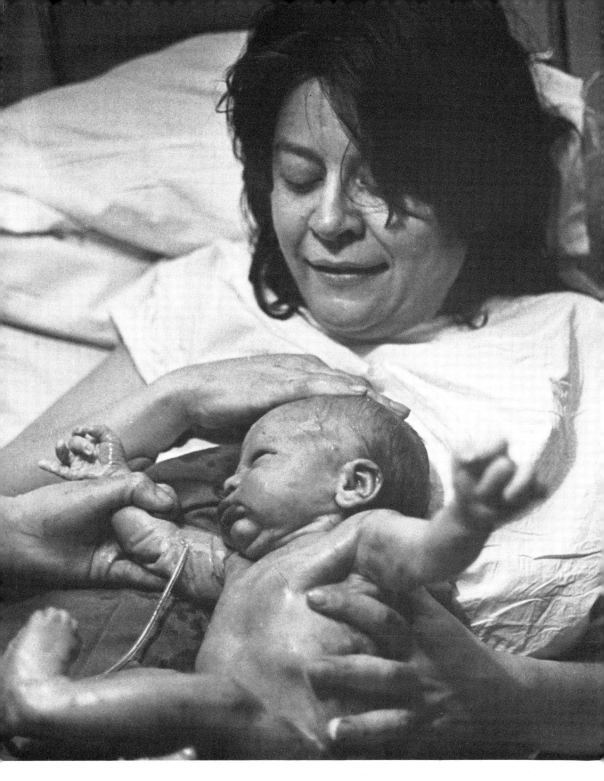

Over the last fifteen years a slow revolution in hospitals has given women an increasing say in how they give birth. Some women, however, still feel there is a long way to go.

Demonstrators in the 1960s protesting against the introduction of the 1967 Act which made abortion legal.

There have also been campaigns to support the millions of Third World women who have been used as guinea pigs in the development of contraceptives, such as those injected – often without their knowledge or consent – with the highly harmful, long-term contraceptive Depo-Provera.

Today, with the spread of the AIDS virus which can be passed on by the exchange of body fluids during sexual intercourse, the question of contraception has an added dimension. Until now, many feminists felt that the so-called 'sexual revolution' of the 1960s, partly facilitated by the pill, made women sexually more available to men, rather than liberating the women themselves. Women who refused casual sex as a 'thank you' for a pleasant evening were accused of being 'frigid' or a virgin. Now, the 'safe sex' guidelines suggest a return to an old standard for sexual morality, namely that sex should be confined to marriage or long-term partnerships.

These campaigns around women's fertility are part of a wider campaign for women to take control of their own health. In *Our Bodies, Our Selves* the Boston Women's Health Collective wrote a self-help guide to good health for women which has become an international best-seller. Women have formed health groups to practise techniques of self-diagnosis and set up 'well-woman' clinics to help women stay healthy.

One of the health problems women face is PMS or premenstrual syndrome, which makes many women feel anxious, depressed or murderously angry once a month and which doctors have tended to dismiss as 'women's troubles'. Another is cancer of the cervix. Currently there is a dispute about a new computerised system to ensure every woman over twenty has a cervical smear once in five years. The Women's National Cancer Control Campaign feels that five years is too long. Many cases of cervical cancer are going undetected, resulting in the deaths of 2000 women in Britain every year.

Women demonstrating outside the House of Commons in the autumn of 1987 against David Alton's Bill which proposed a reduction in the time-limit for abortions from 28 weeks of pregnancy to 18 weeks.

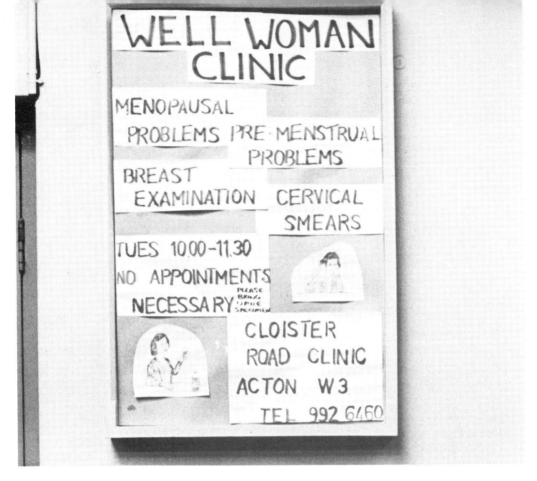

A notice in a Well Woman Clinic showing the range of services on offer.

Over 10 million tranquillizers are taken every day by women in Britain. This is not just because mothers socially isolated at home all day with small children tend to become depressed. Often doctors prescribe valium because they themselves are harassed and over-worked and do not have time to listen to women's complaints. Sometimes actual menstrual or other physical disorders go undiagnosed because the symptoms – like constant pressure, low-level pain or fatigue – are vague enough to allow the doctor to fall back on the age-old advice to women: 'It's all in the mind, dear. Take these for a while and we'll see if it doesn't just go away.'

In 1970 it was calculated that one woman in six in England and Wales would enter hospital because of psychiatric illness at some time in her life, compared with one in nine men. In the 'Social Origins of Depression,' a study of women in Camberwell found that there were usually social or economic reasons for women becoming depressed. They also established that women who had a job outside the home were far less likely to become psychiatrically ill. So perhaps working mothers are more likely to be happy and healthy than full-time mothers.

Case Study 3:

Rosie, aged 18

Soon after she left school and started work, on the cash desk at a new superstore, Rosie started going out with Don, who was a trainee store manager and quite a bit older than her. Now they have been together for two years and plan to get married when they can get a place together.

One of the things which made Don so special, Rosie reflected, was that he was always considerate. He hadn't just pushed her into sex, but had asked her if she felt ready for it and what she thought they should do about contraception. Rosie had heard a lot about the pill from older friends. They complained of putting on weight, being depressed and losing interest in sex altogether. And one of the women at work had a sister who had had a thrombosis, and she was only twenty-six! Rosie did not like the sound of the pill, but she and Don agreed that she should go to the Family Planning Clinic and get some advice about the best method. One thing was certain – they didn't want to start a family yet – not until they were well established and had a house.

The doctor at the clinic seemed very friendly at first, though Rosie felt slight embarrassed talking to a man about it. He suggested that the pill was best because she could be absolutely sure of not getting pregnant. When Rosie told him the bad things she had heard about it, the doctor said: 'Come on now, let's not get hysterical'. In the end he agreed to let her try something different, and arranged for her to come in with Don and have a coil fitted. He said it was perfectly safe. The great thing was you didn't have to remember to take a pill or anything like that. Once it was in, that was it.

The fitting had been very painful, and as she said to Don later, 'the pain doesn't seem to have gone, it's like having period pains all month.' When she went back to the clinic, though, the doctor said it would settle down. It wasn't just the pain, either, she felt run down and exhausted the whole time. She struggled on for a while before going to her own GP about it. He said she had an infection of the fallopian tubes, prescribed very strong antibiotics and gave her two weeks off work. When she was better he agreed she would have to have the coil removed, although he was quite sure that was not what had caused the infection. Perhaps she should try the cap next, or else let Don use condoms.

Would you be more careful if it was you that got pregnant?

Anyone married or single can get advice on contraception from the Family Planning Association.
Margaret Pyke House, 27-35 Mortimer Street, London W1 N 8BQ. Tel. 01-636 9135.

The Health Education Council

A humorous poster with a serious message. Many boys and young men still believe that contraception is the woman's responsibility.

---

1   *Do you think Rosie's experience would have been any different if the Family Planning doctor had been a woman?*
2   *Should girls and women carry condoms and insist that their partners wear them to protect themselves against AIDS as well as unwanted pregnancy? Who do you think should be responsible for contraception? The girl or the boy?*
3   *What is your view on abortion? Should it be freely available? Up to how many weeks into pregnancy? When do you think life begins? And is the right to life of the foetus more important than the mother's rights?*

Tell a story of your own, or one you have heard from a friend, about experiences at the doctor's. Have you ever been made to feel that you are imagining your symptoms?

Images of Women

Women are confronted every day of their lives with stereotypes of how they should be. Basically, these fall into two categories. The first includes the many women on TV quiz or variety shows who are there simply to look decorative while handing out prizes or holding something for the (male) presenter, as well as page three girls in the *Sun* and women as sex objects in advertisements and girlie magazines. The second stereotype is the 'good woman', the virtuous, long-suffering wife and mother who upholds family morality and faithfulness, but who is likely to be boring and bossy with it. She may appear glamorous too, in TV advertisements for soap powder or breakfast cereals, but even when she does, neither she nor her environment is half as mouth-wateringly enticing as that of the bronzed and beautiful bikini-clad girl on the beach advertising beer or shampoo.

Many women object to being confronted with images of women as sex objects or as the subjects of romantic fantasy. Even women who make a living from their bodies have little respect for the men who get enjoyment from looking at these images.

TV domestic sitcoms and indeed much humour depends on using stereotypes. Often the two caricatures of women are opposed for comic effect: nagging wife or domineering mother-in-law confronts blonde and 'available' young secretary. And no matter how dull or boring the man is, the comedy rests on the assumption that he is worth fighting over. So, in most TV drama, women only appear in relationship to a man, not as independent personalities.

Recent examples of the two stereotypes in TV advertisements include the sex symbol sheathed in black satin, bits of whose curvy form and moist red lips in close-up are used to sell a brand of car wax! A 'comic' building society advertisement shows a man desperately fleeing a determined pursuer who is 'after his money' and attempting to run him down in a sinister sleek black limousine. He begs a mate on a building site to shelter him. Mate asks: 'Is it Meatcleaver Kevin, or Ron the Razor?' 'Worse', gasps the terrorized fugitive, 'It's the wife.'

How can this situation be changed? A recent Channel Four programme called 'Putting Women in the Picture' highlighted the problems. In 'The Missing Culture' the Labour Party documents how much men still dominate British culture.

Some advertisements are so offensive to women that they provoke an angry response from them.

Members of the audience at the 1986 Miss World Contest poring over pictures of the contestants. Pressure from the Women's Movement has led to beauty contests being given a lower profile in the media in recent years.

In any one week twice as many men as women appear on TV programmes. And many programmes such as 'Last of the Summer Wine', or 'The Two Ronnies', feature no women at all. When women are asked to be interviewed or to appear on a chat show, it is made clear to them that their make-up, hairstyle, what they wear are of paramount importance. This means that it is hard for middle-aged women to appear on TV. In contrast, grey hair is seen as a definite plus for male presenters, giving them an air of authority. There are twice as many male presenters as women in any week's viewing. Few women are political, defence, or current affairs presenters or reporters. It is only a few years since a top BBC executive said: 'Women cannot read the news, because if women read the news, no one will believe the news.'

Some countries, like Canada, are attempting to change things by portraying women in a wide range of roles, and by ensuring that there is a balance of women to men in each programme. The Canadians have found that implementing this policy has increased the number of viewers.

Many young women model themselves on images they find in magazines.

British women in TV point out that to give women equality of opportunity in the media it will be necessary not only to increase the number of women actors, presenters, and even script writers, but to use female camera people, producers and directors who would give a different perspective of women and men. And more women TV executives might alter programme priorities. Currently, the BBC has no woman on the board of management, no woman in the news directorate, and no woman controller or director.

1   *MP Clare Short tried unsuccessfully to have a Bill passed in Parliament banning page three girls as degrading to women. But Samantha Fox, one of the page three topless models, says 'it's all good, clean fun'. Who do you think is right?*
2   *Why do you think so many stories for teenagers depicting first experiences of love and sexuality have girls as their main characters? Don't boys need fictional models to learn from and identify with?*
3   *Does the mum shown in television ads seem anything like your mum? Why do you think mothers are shown like this on television?*
4   *A Conservative politician described Labour's concern about male domination in British culture as feminism gone mad'. Do you agree?*

Violence Against Women

The issue of rape has been given prominence by the media and the police. Rape crisis centres and women's self-defence classes have had plenty of publicity. Yet women are still afraid to walk in the street at night. Why is this so? Surely women's rights must include the right to exist and to walk around without fear of attack?

What has made rape such a common crime? Feminists think the idea that women are there to gratify men's sexual needs and can be forced to do so is deeply rooted in the way men and women are traditionally supposed to relate to each other. The way the media and the courts deal with rape cases often illustrates this. The idea that a woman is somehow at least partially to blame for what happens to her when she is raped is still very widely accepted. Police and lawyers often argue that the way the woman was dressed, her behaviour, the very fact that she was walking home late at night or hitchhiking mean that she was 'asking for it'.

A 'Women Reclaim the Night' demonstration in Soho, London. Women want the right to be able to go out at night without being considered 'fair game' for sexual harassment and attack.

Nor does there seem to be agreement about how women should react when threatened with sexual assault. If they put up little resistance they are sometimes accused of 'going along with it', 'meaning yes when they say no', or actually enjoying it. Feminist research has made it clear that women may not resist a sex attack because they are afraid for their lives. Rapists often emphasize their verbal and physical threats with a knife or a gun. On the other hand, women who do give in to their attacker are sometimes considered sensible. In a recent case, police praised a girl for her calm passivity: 'After being kidnapped she did just as her attacker told her. As a result she is still around and has been able to help us greatly in the hunt for this man.'

The way rape is reported gives the impression that rapists are in some way 'sick' and therefore different from most men. In the case of a twenty-two-year-old who threatened to kill an eighty-year-old widow before raping her, the man's lawyer said in his defence that 'There was no previous evidence of his having any sexual deviations.' But research has shown that rapes are not only committed by men who are in some way perverted or abnormal, but often by men women know: friends, fathers, lovers and husbands. Increased publicity around child sexual abuse has brought out into the open how widespread the problem of incest is. This childhood experience severely emotionally cripples those women who have suffered it.

A Women's Refuge in North London. Recent FBI statistics show that in the USA four women are beaten to death every day by their husbands or lovers.

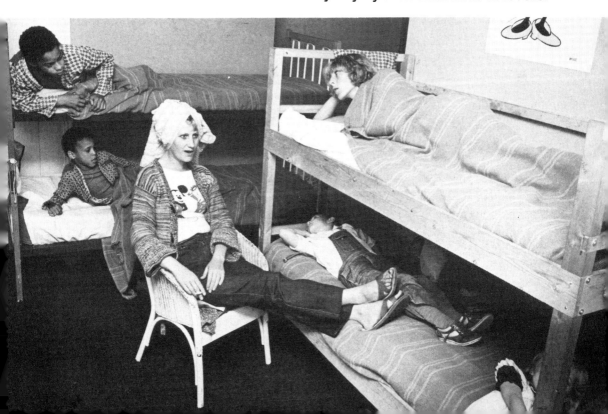

Self-defence classes for women have been set up all over the country to teach women how to protect themselves against physical attack.

In the past, the police have taken the view that a woman who calls for help when her husband has beaten her is the victim of a 'private, domestic dispute' in which they cannot intervene. And social workers took the same view. Then, in 1971 Erin Pizzey set up Women's Aid and the first women's refuge in Chiswick. Now there are refuges for battered women in many countries all over the world.

One of the puzzles is why women often leave the refuge and return to their violent home-life. Women's Aid has made it clear that they often have no alternative. Without paid work they are financially dependent on their husbands. And Social Services does not count them as homeless if they have left home voluntarily. The Women's Aid Federation has succeeded in having some laws changed to help women who try to leave their violent husbands. But changes in the law do not solve everything. There is still no answer to the question of why men rape and beat women. Nor is there yet a way of ensuring a woman's right to live without the threat of physical violence being made or used against her.

Case Study 4:

Liz, aged 37

'It had been an exhausting day at the office, and going straight to the meeting from work had finished me off. By the time I came out of the tube it was already after eleven o'clock and the streets were fairly empty. But it wasn't far to my flat, so I set off to walk, cursing my high-heeled sandals with their narrow straps cutting into my ankles.

Suddenly I became aware of another pair of footsteps behind me and quickened my steps, painfully aware of the stupid sandals. If it were someone following me, there was no way I could run.

I crossed over the road but the footsteps followed me. I glanced round involuntarily, and in that moment he grabbed my arm. 'Hey, beautiful, why the hurry?' I tried to pull my arm free, saying: 'Let me go.' We were right next to some billboards in front of an empty site round the corner from my flat. I looked around frantically for help, but saw no-one. 'Don't scream, or I'll kill you,' he said, suddenly poking a knife in my face. His tone and threatening look made me feel he meant it as he yanked me behind the billboard and pushed me to the ground. He clamped his hand over my mouth and pinned me down with all his weight. I still can't talk about what happened, even to my best friend. I wake up bolt upright with fear every night.

After he left me lying there, bruised and shaking, I managed to get myself the last few yards home, feeling numb with shock and horror. I couldn't even cry. I got into the bath and tried to wash off the feeling of being unclean. I couldn't sleep, and next day stayed off work. I just lay in bed all day, crying. The thoughts pounded endlessly through my head: what if I had walked home the other way? Would there have been more people around? Was it my fault for wearing such silly sandals? I couldn't get rid of the feeling that I was somehow to blame.

I never went to the police. The thought of having to go through it all again was more than I could bear. And I had heard awful stories about the way they treat you – making you feel you had 'asked for it'. They would have wanted to know all about my sex life, and because I didn't have a permanent relationship, they might have implied that I had wanted the sex. It has really affected the way I feel about men. I'm not even sure I want a relationship now. As for sex – I just don't really enjoy it. It makes me sick and disgusted. I feel as if nothing will ever be the same again – and yet it's over a year since it happened.'

The police have made efforts to improve the quality of the treatment they give to rape victims. This picture, from a video film, shows a specially trained policewoman comforting a rape victim (played by an actress).

1 How do you think Liz should have acted? Would it have made any difference to what happened?
2 Some police authorities now refer rape victims to counselling and support schemes. Do you think more women will feel able to report cases of sexual assault as a result?
3 'Video nasties have a lot to answer for in the rising tide of sexual violence against women'. Discuss this view.

Recently, newspapers reported the case of a teenage girl who was taken down to the beach for sex by a man she met at a club. When she was found naked after the man had abandoned her because he 'had a bus to catch', she claimed she had been raped. The girl was sent to youth custody for ninety days after admitting she had 'made a false claim' and 'wasted police time'. Is this a case of sexual abuse, or not? Discuss.

All Change

What has changed for women? Do they have more rights today than fifty or 100 years ago? Some people feel that the Women's Liberation Movement has changed not only women's consciousness, but attitudes in general. A woman has a right to keep her own name after marriage, to be separately taxed from her husband, and, if the marriage breaks down, to stay in the family home until the youngest child is sixteen. But equal pay is still a myth for most women and the 4 million women part-timers do not have equal employment rights. Despite a promise by the Conservative Party in the early 1970s that they would provide enough nursery school places to equal demand by the mid-1980s, it is still only the lucky few who can get their children into a nursery school. Women may be reporting rape more often than in the past, but is this because they feel they will get a fair hearing from the police, or does it simply reflect an increase in the number of rapes?

Mrs Jacqueline Drake claimed the DHSS was discriminating against married women by refusing to pay them an allowance for looking after invalid relatives at home. She took her case to the European Court of Justice. Subsequently the rules have been changed so that thousands of women are now receiving payment.

Some of the 30,000 people, mainly women, who linked hands along the fourteen-kilometre perimeter fence to 'embrace' the Greenham Common Cruise Missile base on 12 December, 1982.

Some people feel that we are still fighting for the same things our mothers and grandmothers fought for. Certainly many other European countries, both East and West, have better provisions for implementing women's rights. France, West Germany and New Zealand all have a Ministry for Women but the present British government has often directly opposed moves to extend women's rights. For example, in 1982 it vetoed a draft EEC directive designed to give part-timers equal rights with full-timers, such as they already enjoy in Sweden.

European Community legislation on women's rights has on occasion been used to take cases of discrimination to the European Court of Justice. As a result of a ruling in February 1986 in the Helen Marshall case it is now unlawful in the public sector in Britain to force women to retire earlier than men. The European Commission also took legal action to make the British government update its Sex Discrimination Act with a new Bill in 1986.

Martina Navratilova, for many years the number one women's tennis player in the world. Despite the popularity of women's tennis, women who win get less in prize money than male tennis stars.

How is change brought about? Some people still feel – despite the shortcomings of the Equal Pay Act and the Sex Discrimination Act, and the limitations to the powers of the Equal Opportunities Commission – that the only way to change things is by changing the law and changing institutions. A substantial number of women have moved into the established political parties. This is reflected in the record number of women MPs elected in 1987. In 1981, with only 3 per cent of the total 635 seats in Parliament (8 Conservative and 11 Labour women MPs), women had fewer representatives in parliament than at any time since before the Second World War. Now there are 41 women MPs (21 Labour and 17 Conservative, 2 Alliance and 1 SNP), accounting for 6.3 per cent of parliamentary seats. This is still a small number of women compared with East Germany where women fill 32 per cent of seats in the Volkskammer, but it does compare favourably with the US House of Representatives in which only 5 per cent of the members are women. In Iceland the founding of the Women's Party resulted in an increased number of seats for women in the 1987 election.

Despite the increasing number of women in trade unions, there are very few women delegates at the annual Trades Union Congress.

Women's Centres have been established all over the country. The Camden Women's Bus shown here provided a mobile centre where women could meet and seek advice and support from each other.

Some women continue to feel that it is more effective to campaign around a single issue, and in women-only groups. A good example is the women's peace movement which has given women a sense both of being able to take control of their lives and of trying to ensure a peaceful future. The Greenham peace women have had an impact worldwide. They have become a symbol for non-violent ways of changing things. Women at meetings decide who is to be the facilitator (chair) and note-taker; there are no fixed officers like chairperson or secretary. Everyone takes a turn at the responsible jobs, and everyone is listened to. The way Greenham women have talked with police and soldiers at the base has become a model of non-violent political action.

Whether in the organized structures of political power or outside them, it is only when women take action to control their own lives that things change. There are many ways of campaigning for women's rights and much is still to be done.

Helpful Organizations

British Pregnancy Advisory Service
Head office:
Austy Manor
Wootten Wawen
Solihull
B95 6BX
Tel: (05642) 3225
For regional offices, contact the head office.

Family Planning Clinic
See your local telephone directory or ask directory enquiries. The FPC will provide free contraception and give advice on matters relating to sex and health.

Low Pay Unit
9 Upper Berkeley Street
London W1H 8BY
Tel: 01–262 7278

Rape Crisis Centre
See your local telephone directory or ask directory enquiries. Most centres have a 24-hour telephone number.

Rights for Women Unit
National Council for Civil Liberties
(NCCL)
186 Kings Cross Road
London WC1X 9DE
Tel: 01–403 3888

The Equal Opportunities Commission
Overseas House
Quay Street
Manchester M3 3HN
Tel: (061) 833 9244

Women's Research and Resources
Centre and Feminist Library
Hungerford House
Victoria Embankment
London WC2N 6PA
Tel: 01–930 0715
Opening hours: Wed, Fri and Sat: 11.00–5.30; Thurs: 11.00–7.30

Acknowledgements

The publishers would like to thank the following for providing the illustrations in this book: Camera Press 4 (Cosmo Werner), 8, 9, 12, 26, 30, 41 (Homer Sykes); Format, cover and 5 (Brenda Prince), 13 (Pam Isherwood), 17, 19 and 20 (Brenda Prince), 21 (Michael Ann Mullen), 22 (Raissa Page), 28 (Maggie Murray), 31 (Jenny Matthews), 33 (Joanne O'Brien), 35 (Val Wilmer), 36 (Maggie Murray), 37 (Pam Isherwood), 42 (Maggie Murray), 43 (Sheila Gray), 44 (Pam Isherwood); Richard and Sally Greenhill 15, 16; *Guardian* 6 (Denis Thorpe); Network 25 and 27 (John Sturrock); Jill Posener 32; Topham 7, 11, 23, 39, 40.

Glossary

Abortion The ending of a pregnancy.

Birth control pill A pill taken to prevent pregnancy.

Caesarian birth When a baby is born through an incision in the mother's abdomen.

Cervical smear The removal of cells from the cervix in order to test them for cancer.

Cervix Where the womb opens into the vagina.

Condom (or sheath) A form of contraceptive which is fitted over the penis before sexual intercourse.

Contraceptive Device used to prevent pregnancy resulting from sexual intercourse.

Demob (demobilise) Release a soldier from the army.

Diaphragm (or cap) A form of contraceptive which is placed over the cervix before sexual intercourse.

Discriminate Single out a person, or group of people, on the basis of sex, colour, or belief.

Dutch cap See Diaphragm.

Exploit Take advantage of a person, usually one in a weaker position.

Gay rights The right of homosexuals not to be discriminated against.

Oppress Force a person to behave in a servile fashion.

Lesbian A woman who prefers to have sexual relations with women.

Maternity leave A period of time off work taken by a woman when she is having a child and after which she has the right to return to her job (or a similar one).

Redundancy pay Money given by an employer to people who lose their jobs through no fault of their own.

Sexual harassment The tormenting of a person (usually female) by another person (usually male). It can take many forms, from personal comments about the person's appearance or sexuality, to requests or demands for sexual intercourse.

Sick pay Money paid either by an employer or the State to a person who is unable to work because of illness.

Stereotype A fixed idea about a person or group of people.

Suffrage The right to vote.

Further Reading

Against Our Will by Susan Brownmiller (Penguin, 1976)

All That: The Other Half of History by Kate Charlesworth and Marsali Cameron (Pandora Press, 1986)

A Woman's Place by Morag Alexander (Wayland, 1983)

Boxed In: Women in Television edited by Helen Baehr and Gillian Dyer (Pandora Press, 1987)

Georgie Porgie: Sexual Harassment in Everyday Life by Sue Wise and Liz Stanley (Pandora Press, 1987)

Feminism for Girls: An Adventure Story edited by Angela McRobbie and Trisha McCabe (Routledge and Kegan Paul, 1981)

Getting There: Job Hunting for Women by Margaret Wallis (Kogan Page, 1987)

Greenham Common: Women at the Wire edited by Barbara Harford and Sarah Hopkins (The Women's Press, 1984)

Hidden from History by Sheila Rowbotham (Pluto Press, 1972)

One Hand Tied Behind Us: The Rise of the Women's Suffrage Movement by Jill Liddington and Jill Norris (Virago, 1978)

Our Bodies, Our Selves: A Health Book by and for Women (Penguin, 1978)

Our Work, Our Lives, Our Words edited by Leonore Davidson and Belinda Westover (Macmillan, 1986)

Sexual Harassment at Work by Ann Sedley and Melissa Benn (NCCL, 1982)

Subject Women by Ann Oakley (Fontana, 1982)

The Rape Controversy by Melissa Benn, Anna Coote and Tess Gill (NCCL, 1986)

The Role of Women by Sharon Goulds (Macdonald, 1985)

Typical Girls by Christine Griffin (Pandora Press, 1985)

Women by Eileen McConnell (Batsford, 1982)

Women's Health: A Spare Rib Reader by Sue O'Sullivan (Pandora Press, 1987)

Women History Makers series (Macdonald)

Women in History series (Wayland)

Women on the Line by Ruth Cavendish (Routledge and Kegan Paul, 1982)

Women Workers and the Trade Unions by Sarah Boston (Lawrence and Wishart, 1987)

Autobiography and Fiction

A Woman by Sibilla Aleramo (Virago, 1979)

Girls are Powerful: Young Women's Writings from Spare Rib edited by Susan Hemmings (Sheba, 1982)

Cry Hard and Swim: The Story of an Incest Survivor by Jacqueline Spring (Virago, 1987)

Forever by Judy Blume (Pan, 1986)

More to Life than Mr Right: Stories for Young Feminists compiled by Rosemary Stones (Fontana, 1987)

My Brilliant Career by Miles Franklin (Virago, 1980)

Push Me, Pull Me by Sandra Check (The Women's Press, 1987)

The Colour Purple by Alice Walker (Women's Press, 1983)

Three Guineas by Virginia Woolf (Penguin, 1979)

Wayward Girls and Wicked Women edited by Angela Carter (Virago, 1986)

Index